A Practical Guide to Prairie Reconstruction

A BUR OAK BOOK | *Holly Carver, series editor*

A PRACTICAL GUIDE TO

PRAIRIE
RECONSTRUCTION

SECOND EDITION

Carl Kurtz

University of Iowa Press, Iowa City

University of Iowa Press, Iowa City 52242
Copyright © 2013 by Carl Kurtz
www.uiowapress.org
Printed in the United States of America

Design by Kristina Kachele Design, llc

The University of Iowa Press is a member of Green Press Initiative
and is committed to preserving natural resources.

Printed on acid-free paper
Library of Congress Cataloging-in-Publication Data

Kurtz, Carl.
A practical guide to prairie reconstruction / by Carl Kurtz.—2nd ed.
p. cm.—(A Bur oak book)
Includes bibliographical references.
ISBNS 978-1-60938-168-4, 1-60938-168-8 (pbk.)
ISBNS 978-1-60938-173-8, 1-60938-173-4 (e-book)
1. Prairie restoration—Iowa. 2. Prairie planting—Iowa.
3. Prairie plants—Iowa. I. Title. II. Series: Bur oak book.
S621.5.G73K87 2013
639.9'909777—dc23   2012043132

Page ii photographs (*clockwise from top left*):
⁜ The black swallowtail seen here on Culver's root is often a common butterfly during the summer months.
⁜ Sedge wren on a flowering compass plant in a twenty-year-old prairie reconstruction.
⁜ A dense stand of pale purple coneflower, black-eyed Susan, and round-headed bush-clover in a thirty-year-old prairie reconstruction.

Page iii photograph:
⁜ Rattlesnake master, compass plant, and showy tick-trefoil in a fifteen-year-old prairie reconstruction.

To all prairie enthusiasts who are working to save, reconstruct, and restore the tallgrass prairie

⌃ Prairie blazing star, purple prairie clover, and large leaves of
compass plants in a thirty-year-old prairie reconstruction.

CONTENTS

< Midsummer tallgrass prairie with compass plant and showy tick-trefoil in full flower.

◁ Bobolinks are common nesters in tallgrass prairie. This bird is perched on butterfly weed in a remnant piece of virgin tallgrass prairie.

A Practical Guide to Prairie Reconstruction

CHAPTER ONE

INTRODUCTION

What was the tallgrass prairie? Why should we care about reconstructing it today?
What will this guide accomplish?

No living person today remembers Iowa when tallgrass prairie—a highly diverse community of drought-tolerant grasses, sedges, and wildflowers—stretched from the Mississippi to the Missouri River. Botanist Daryl Smith has written that nearly all of Iowa's original prairie disappeared in the seventy years between 1830 and 1900, when settlers moved into the state. Most of North America's 224,000 square miles of tallgrass prairie had met a similar fate by 1930.

⋀ An open prairie landscape in early summer with building cumulus clouds
and a lone bur oak on an eighteen-year-old prairie reconstruction.

By 1910 most of Iowa's 28 million acres of tallgrass prairie, more than 80 percent of the state's total land area, had either been plowed under or would eventually be destroyed by overgrazing. Today less than 2 percent of Iowa's original tallgrass prairie exists as relicts along roadsides and railroad rights-of-way and in old cemeteries and state preserves. Although some people still view prairie plants as weeds, a growing number are committed to bringing tallgrass prairie back to the Midwest.

In this newly revised edition of *A Practical Guide to Prairie Reconstruction*, as in the first edition, I outline the procedures and problems that you may face in the process of reconstructing a tallgrass prairie, whether it be in your backyard or on your back forty.

The term "reconstruction" means starting prairie from scratch in a bare crop field. "Restoration" is the process of reclaiming grasslands that have been degraded from heavy grazing or lack of management but that still retain remnant populations of native prairie plant species. Both processes require restoring a diversity of native grasses, sedges, and forbs (a collective name for prairie flowers) and implementing

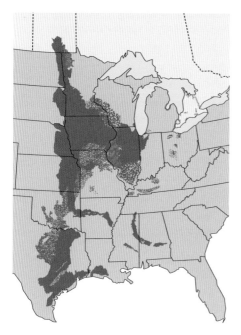

a management plan. This guide will not answer every possible question, since each planting is unique, but it should provide a formula for success under most conditions, even in a very dry year. I have updated all the original chapters, the list of seed sources and services, and the references; replaced the original photos with new photos; and added new chapters covering herbicide use and the procedure for restoring old pastures.

We live on a family farm in central Iowa that was purchased by my father in 1930. It was operated as a typical diverse grain and livestock operation until about 1970. As a wildlife biologist, I wanted to resurrect an old pasture that was severely eroded from

⌃ In the early nineteenth century, tallgrass prairie occupied the eastern portion of midcontinental North America between the mixed-grass prairie and the eastern deciduous forest. Today less than 2 to 3 percent of the original prairie remains. Map used courtesy of Brent Butler, Daryl Smith, and the Tallgrass Prairie Center.

overgrazing. In 1975, working with our county conservation board, we planted to a mix of five prairie grass species: big bluestem, little bluestem, side-oats grama, Indian grass, and switchgrass. This planting protected the soil and provided wildlife habitat, but over a ten-year period I realized that without forb diversity, the planting lacked long-term stability.

In 1988 my wife and partner, Linda, and I began planting cropland to local-ecotype seed in the hope that it would provide superior wildlife habitat, protect the soil from erosion, and produce farm income from the sale of native ecotype prairie seed. Unforeseen benefits included a dramatic improvement in soil structure and the restoration of water quality in a small wetland located in one of the reconstructed areas.

While most prairie reconstructions begin with the establishment of warm-season grasses, nature always works toward diversity. Grasslands without prairie flowers (broadleaf plants) have empty root spaces. Nature's mission is to fill in that empty space with whatever is available. If a diversity of prairie forbs is present, they will do the job. If these are absent, weedy and often undesirable species such as Canada thistle will move in. A plant community with a higher diversity of species will have greater stability.

The process of reconstructing and restoring prairie grasslands has made great strides in the past twenty-five-plus years. If land and resources are available, it is now possible to plant a prairie with more than a hundred species that function as dynamically as any natural system. This is especially important since we live in a world filled with introduced species from around the globe, better known to most land managers as invasive species. There is growing evidence that these species invade natural areas more readily where there is low species diversity. Removing them is a costly, time-consuming process and in many cases is not even possible.

Tallgrass prairie is critical wildlife habitat as well as an important element in flood control and stream water treatment. There is growing evidence that prairie stream buffers stop soil loss, while created wetlands remove unwanted nutrients from run-off and tile water. The social and economic benefits of these reconstructions may be critical for future generations.

We hope that this guide provides basic directions and encouragement for individuals with private property as well as for land managers working with government agencies and nonprofit organizations who have taken up the task of reconstructing and restoring native grasslands.

We are deeply indebted to numerous individuals who have worked with us over the past thirty-seven-plus years. They have shared their stories and asked countless questions that have helped us understand the process of reconstruction and restoration of the tallgrass prairie. Interns working with us in our plantings have helped make them remarkably weed-free. Friends have faithfully helped with our seed-bagging operation each fall, while prairie enthusiasts have purchased our seed. This has given us the opportunity to make a modest living while refining the process for success under a broad range of field conditions.

CHAPTER TWO

IDENTIFICATION

What does today's tallgrass prairie look like? Where can you find one?
What plants does it contain throughout the season?

In order to understand what a prairie is, we first need to define it. The word "prairie" has many meanings. Some consider it an open landscape where the horizon is generally visible in all directions. Whether this landscape is planted to grass, grain, or indigenous vegetation is of little consequence. The word "prairie" may still have other meanings, but for the purpose of this guide, let us consider the definition of tallgrass prairie as follows.

⌃ An example of a virgin prairie. Doolittle pothole prairie with
prairie blazing star, gray-headed coneflower, and compass plant.

The best examples of remaining tallgrass prairie today are generally referred to as virgin prairie. From a botanical perspective, virgin prairie is a complex plant association that has not been plowed to raise cultivated crops or overgrazed to eliminate most native species. The plant community in this type of prairie developed over several thousands of years and was generally devoid of trees except where there were natural barriers such as rivers, streams, and marshes. Mixed- and shortgrass prairies grew in response to decreased annual rainfall and begin somewhat west of the Missouri River, or the 100th meridian, and extend to the foothills of the Rocky Mountains.

Virgin prairies differ from planted grasslands and open-country pastures because they possess a wide diversity of native grasses, sedges, and forbs. Most plants are perennials: they come up from the same root system year after year using energy reserves stored from the year before. Roots vary in depth and size from species like prairie violets, which may be only a few inches in depth, to compass plants that may be a foot across at the crown and more than ten feet in length. Unlike planted grasslands and pastures, which may contain up to thirty species (but usually have far fewer), most virgin prairies have two to three hundred species in a complex association. The actual number of species depends on slope, soil type, and available moisture.

Virgin prairies often possess a wide array of animals adapted to open areas. The meadowlark and bobolink are typical prairie birds. Bison and elk are typical prairie mammals displaced by settlement.

Keep in mind that this definition of prairie is only to facilitate your understanding of tallgrass prairie reconstruction. In order to reconstruct tallgrass prairie, you should become familiar with the grasses and forbs in a tallgrass remnant. Start by visiting a selected site at least once a month from April through November. If you are unfamiliar with a virgin prairie site in your area, contact your local county conservation board, state conservation officer, garden club, your state chapter of The Nature Conservancy, or the Audubon Society.

The plants of spring are usually short; as the season progresses, later-blooming forbs and grasses are taller. In spring a tallgrass prairie may be only six inches to one foot high. By midsummer it will likely be between three and four feet high, and by late summer some grasses and flowers will be seven feet high or greater. Exceptions to this are species like bottle gentians and ladies'-tresses, which flower during early September at a height of six to eighteen inches, respectively.

Early in the season, there is little color in the dried brown grasses remaining on a prairie landscape. Pasque flowers can be found in the northern half of Iowa and begin to bloom in early April. In late April or early May, you can find a miniature sunflower called golden ragwort, the demure blossoms of blue-eyed grass, and yellow stargrass. The latter two are members of the iris and daffodil families, respectively. Also seen at this time of year is wood betony, which has a twisted head of yellow tubular flowers and soft, fernlike leaves. The flowers of prairie violets are similar in size and shape to those of common blue violets; however, prairie violet leaves are deeply dissected. Later in May, shooting stars can be found.

In late spring, the orange phloxlike blossoms of hoary puccoon and prairie phlox grow among the slender stems of porcupine grass. Porcupine grass, a cool-season species, is also known as needle grass. Its needle-tipped seeds have a long awn that corkscrews as it dries, planting the seed. Canada wild rye is also a cool-season grass that flowers in late spring. Some varieties have bluish leaves that are wider at the base than most other grasses. The seed head, as the name implies, reminds one of rye or wheat.

In late June and early July, the prairie celebration gets into full swing. Black-eyed Susan, pale purple coneflower, and butterfly weed add bursts of color. In late July and August, the warm-season grasses such as little bluestem and side-oats grama begin to flower. On dry slopes, little bluestem intermingles with the striking magenta of rough blazing star. Along mesic (moist) swales, you can often find prairie blazing star, compass plant, and common mountain mint. The leaves, stems, and flowers of mountain mint have tiny oil glands that give the plant a pungent smell when crushed. Big bluestem, also called turkey foot, may attain a height of seven to nine feet in late August. Indian grass and switchgrass extend to their full height and flower in late summer. In early autumn, the deep blue of bottle gentian, which is pollinated only by bumblebees, can be found in swales. Downy gentians favor the drier upland of rich mesic prairies.

Many species of sunflowers, asters, and goldenrods bring up parade's end in September and early October, some flowering well after the first autumn frost. Tall goldenrod, with a plumelike flower head, and stiff goldenrod, with a flat-topped flower head, are two of the most common species. Four species of asters are often abundant in central Iowa. Heath aster has dense masses of tiny white flowers. Smooth aster, as the name implies, has a smooth stem and sky-blue flowers. The white flowers of frost aster are perhaps an inch across and not as densely grouped as those of heath aster. New England aster, which has deep blue or light magenta flowers, likes wet swales and is often found in gardens.

While this is only a sprinkling of the number of species found across Iowa, many occur across the Midwest and are good indicators of native prairie vegetation.

It is not possible to learn all the prairie plants in a single season, a dozen seasons, or even a lifetime. If you begin to look at prairies in your area, you will find that common species are easily identified—and with recognition comes the constant pleasure of seeing old friends in prairie relicts throughout the countryside.

CHAPTER THREE

SEED SELECTION AND HARVEST

Why use seed rather than live plants? How many species should you plant?
Where should you obtain the seed?

Seeding a prairie, as opposed to planting with live plants, is the only economical way to establish any area larger than a backyard garden. The greatest problem in planting a prairie is obtaining a diverse seed assortment at an economical price.

We have already mentioned in chapter 2 that prairies often contain two to three hundred species in a complex association. However, most nursery catalogs list only seventy to one hundred species with the seed of some species costing two hundred or

⌃ Purple prairie clover, rosinweed, and midsummer grasses
on a sixteen-year-old prairie reconstruction.

more dollars per pound. Is prairie planting actually feasible from an economic point of view?

Research by Robert Betz, a prairie botanist from Northeastern Illinois University, has shown that a relatively small number of a prairie's total species actually comprise a major portion of its standing biomass (the weight or volume of living plants). Thus, a reconstructed prairie can have many features of a virgin prairie with about 10 percent of the total species. This is not to say that the remaining 90 percent are not important, but in many cases they occupy little actual space.

We have had the most success with the species listed on pages 13 and 14. Try to obtain as many of these as possible, and try to use at least thirty species. Many species can be hand-collected in small quantities. Be sure to obtain permission before collecting in any area, and above all do not dig plants from any area unless they are about to be destroyed by development. It is far easier to plant your prairie from seed than from transplants. I have rescued a few plants in the past twenty-five years from abandoned railroad rights-of-way. It was backbreaking work with meager results.

Much has been written about the use of local seed types. A local-ecotype seed is one that naturally evolved on or near your site. Some individuals consider seed to be local only if it is produced within ten miles, others thirty miles, and still others seventy to one hundred miles from your location. Because prairie plants that evolved locally are adapted to the climate of your area, the seeds they produce are certainly the best choice.

Some prairie enthusiasts are very firm about using local-ecotype seed and are concerned that seed from out of state may weaken local genetic stock. Botanists too are especially concerned about genetic purity near state prairie preserves. Because the market for local-ecotype seed is increasing, it appears that more will be produced to meet the demand. When purchasing seed, be sure you know its source origin and whether it is certified for viability by a seed-testing laboratory.

Will seeds that are not locally adapted work in your planting if local-ecotype seed is not available? In older plantings, we used some grass species that were of a western or southern origin. A southwest variety of big bluestem almost completely disappeared fifteen years after planting. In another planting, western little bluestem seems to be quite stable after twelve years. The key to success is having as much variety in

your mix as possible. I believe that species diversity and local-ecotype seed are both very important if your prairie is to have long-term stability. Diversity fills empty root space at all levels, while local-ecotype seed is climatically adapted to the temperature and moisture regime in your area. Seed that originated in dry areas may be suscepti- ble to fungal diseases where there is higher rainfall and subsequent higher humidity.

Ideally the best way to get a large quantity of local-ecotype seed is to harvest it from a virgin prairie remnant using a grass stripper or a small combine. For many years we have harvested part of a twenty-acre virgin prairie with an old Allis-Chalmers pull- type combine. The main modification needed is to block most of the airflow beneath the sieves. This prevents the loss of light, fluffy seeds such as those of goldenrods and asters. Harvesting takes place in the fall when the stems and leaves of the grasses and flowers are dry enough to be thrashed (usually early to mid October in Iowa). The harvested seed mixture will contain broken stems and leaves. Since shattering takes place when the combine reel strikes the seed head, you will not get all the seed from each plant. If there is a slight breeze, seeds of all types will flow freely from the com- bine header and over the tailings sieves. Our best harvests have produced 10 percent seed in bulk mixes from virgin prairie sites. Weather is a big factor, however, and after a very dry and hot summer we have seen the percentage of seed in the mix fall

⌃ Detail of a mixture of prairie grass and forb seed
that is important for a diverse prairie planting.

below 2 percent. Generally we do not process or clean mixed seed. This is labor-intensive work and does not improve seed quality. For best results, store seed in a cool, dry place that is free from mice. Storing seed in jars would be good for mice, but if it was not dry it could mold. If it is in paper bags, any moisture in it will evaporate. We store our seed in brown paper bags or in woven poly-plastic, which breathes.

We have also hand-gathered seeds of species such as prairie phlox, spiked lobelia, flowering spurge, Indian plantain, golden ragwort, and cream gentian and added them to our bulk mixes with good results.

SUGGESTED SPECIES LIST

Common Name	Scientific Name
Big bluestem	*Andropogon gerardii*
Black-eyed Susan	*Rudbeckia hirta*
Bottle gentian	*Gentiana andrewsii*
Butterfly weed	*Asclepias tuberosa*
Canada wild rye	*Elymus canadensis*
Common milkweed	*Asclepias syriaca*
Common mountain mint	*Pycnanthemum virginianum*
Compass plant	*Silphium laciniatum*
Culver's root	*Veronicastrum virginicum*
Cup plant	*Silphium perfoliatum*
Early meadow-rue	*Thalictrum dioicum*
False boneset	*Brickellia eupatorioides*
Golden alexanders	*Zizia aurea*
Gray-headed coneflower	*Ratibida pinnata*
Heath aster	*Aster ericoides*
Hoary vervain	*Verbena stricta*
Indian grass	*Sorghastrum nutans*
Ironweed	*Vernonia fasciculata*
June grass	*Koeleria macrantha*
Leadplant	*Amorpha canescens*
Little bluestem	*Schizachyrium scoparium*
Milk vetch	*Astragalus canadensis*
New England aster	*Aster novae-angliae*
Ox-eye	*Heliopsis helianthoides*
Pale purple coneflower	*Echinacea pallida*
Porcupine grass	*Stipa spartea*
Prairie blazing star	*Liatris pycnostachya*
Prairie cord grass	*Spartina pectinata*
Prairie coreopsis	*Coreopsis palmata*
Prairie dropseed	*Sporobolus heterolepis*
Prairie phlox	*Phlox pilosa*

Common Name	Scientific Name
Prairie spiderwort	*Tradescantia bracteata*
Purple prairie clover	*Dalea purpurea*
Rattlesnake master	*Eryngium yuccifolium*
Rosinweed	*Silphium integrifolium*
Rough blazing star	*Liatris aspera*
Round-headed bush-clover	*Lespedeza capitata*
Saw-tooth sunflower	*Helianthus grosseserratus*
Shooting star	*Dodecatheon meadia*
Showy tick-trefoil	*Desmodium canadense*
Side-oats grama	*Bouteloua curtipendula*
Smooth aster	*Aster laevis*
Sneezeweed	*Helenium autumnale*
Stiff goldenrod	*Solidago rigida*
Swamp milkweed	*Asclepias incarnata*
Switchgrass	*Panicum virgatum*
Tall cinquefoil	*Potentilla arguta*
Tall goldenrod	*Solidago canadensis*
Thimbleweed	*Anemone cylindrica*
Water hemlock	*Cicuta maculata*
Western yarrow	*Achillea millefolium*
White prairie clover	*Dalea candida*
White sage	*Artemisia ludoviciana*
White wild indigo	*Baptisia lactea*
Wild bergamot	*Monarda fistulosa*
Wild rose	*Rosa* species
Winged loosestrife	*Lythrum alatum*

Nomenclature is drawn primarily from *The Vascular Plants of Iowa: An Annotated Checklist and Natural History* by Lawrence J. Eilers and Dean M. Roosa and *The Tallgrass Prairie Center Guide to Prairie Restoration in the Upper Midwest* by Daryl Smith, Dave Williams, Greg Houseal, and Kirk Henderson.

CHAPTER FOUR

SITE SELECTION

How did prairie soils develop? Will prairie plants grow equally well in rich and poor soils?

Prairie soils, which support today's agriculture so successfully, developed over a peri-od of thousands of years. Research by David Montgomery, cited in the July 2008 issue of *Scientific American*, indicates that topsoil formation is a very slow process; it can take from 700 to 1,500 years to form an inch of soil. Before cultivation, the growth and subsequent death of the roots and crowns of prairie plants form humus in the upper soil layers, giving them a dark brown to almost black appearance. Humus mixed with fine clays and sand gives soils the ability to hold water and nutrients and keeps them

⌃ Open, gently rolling landscapes devoid of trees work
best to give your site more opportunities for diversity.

friable (somewhat loose and crumbly). When soil is moist, you can press it between your thumb and forefinger, and it will break apart easily. Virgin prairie soils may have a topsoil layer that extends eighteen inches below the surface.

Plowing of prairies and subsequent agricultural use oxidize the humus, leaving the soils less able to hold water and nutrients. The erosive action of moving water on an unprotected soil surface also removes organic material in the form of silt. Silt floats in a watery suspension and is carried by heavy rains to rivers and streams, where it is deposited in lakes, reservoirs, and quiet river backwaters.

Some prairies started the soil-building process on glacial till, a mixture of rock ground by glacial ice into a flourlike consistency. Other prairies began on loess deposits, which consist of fine wind-blown particles lifted from major river and stream valleys, formed during a period when glaciers were receding.

Prairie vegetation effectively started on very poor soil, which had no topsoil and few nutrients. Prairie plants can become established on very poor soil and survive; however, they do far better where at least some topsoil remains to hold nutrients and water. Prairie plants, like other crops, require nutrients and an adequate water supply to reach maximum height and maturity; thus, their size reflects the quality of the soil.

In 1975, I planted two small areas of prairie flowers and grasses in a borrow ditch along a county road where the topsoil had been completely removed and used for fill. The borrow had been seeded to smooth brome grass by the county road department during the mid 1960s, but the grass was short, thin, and unproductive with bare soil between the plants. After a light disking, I seeded about thirty species, which included three or four grasses and twenty-five forbs. The area remained bare most of the summer, but by the following season many small prairie seedlings began to appear, and gradually over a period of years the plants became well established. Today, more than thirty-five years later, most plants are generally short when compared with similar species on better soil, but only a few small open spaces remain. The plants are also adversely affected by wetter or drier than normal weather conditions. There is still very little or no appreciable topsoil; however, the prairie appears to be well established, and it has virtually halted the erosion that still persists where brome dominates other sections of the road grade.

One of the advantages of planting on poor versus rich soil is a reduction in weedy competition. Very poor soil does not support weeds well and, over the long term, prairie plants are the survivors. In comparison, prairie plantings on rich soil tend to be tall and lush unless the weather conditions are extremely wet or dry; however, initial establishment is more difficult because of weed competition.

Tallgrass prairie plants grow best in full sunlight. Even partial shade may adversely affect a prairie planting. Savanna, a transition zone between open prairie and forest, contains scattered trees. The relatively open yet partially shaded savanna areas often contain cool-season grasses and a number of sedges not common in tallgrass prairie, but some tallgrass species such as Culver's root and rough blazing star also thrive there. The open shade requires many different species to fill this niche. Savanna mixes are available from some seed suppliers.

When you select a site, you should also consider its potential for future management. Will burning be permitted? Will there be future development, which can lead to the introduction of exotic species? Urban plantings are often prone to invasion by exotic legumes such as crown vetch and bird's-foot trefoil and a host of other horticultural urban plants.

CHAPTER FIVE

SOIL PREPARATION

What kind of tillage should you use? Should you use herbicides in addition to tillage?

Planting tallgrass prairie has many similarities to planting a garden or a field crop such as corn, soybeans, oats, or alfalfa. As with gardens and farm crops, it is far easier to start new plants in a weed-free environment. Tallgrass prairie planted by nature before the influence of Euro-American immigrants grew with little competition from weeds. Most alien weeds we know today (especially the annuals) were still at home in Europe. While you should strive for the ideal, few prairies can be planted in weed-free conditions. Soil use over the past hundred years has contaminated most

⌃ Broadcasting a prairie seed mix into drilled soybean stubble or harvested corn stalks in November or later in early winter will expose the forb seed to a process of cold-wet stratification. The undisturbed stubble will prevent wind and water erosion from heavy spring rains.

of the land with weeds. The soil seed bank is full of unwelcome surprises once the growing season starts.

After many years of planting prairie, I feel that if conditions permit, late fall plantings (from late October to mid November) are best, because many species benefit from a period of cold-wet stratification to germinate. If you are planting in a harvested crop field, soybean stubble or corn stubble makes an excellent seedbed. Simply plant directly into the stubble without tillage; rain and snow will plant your seed. Herbicide use has replaced cultivation in most crop fields; however, if they have been cultivated and contain ridges, mowing the planting will be difficult. A light disking will level the field, but disturbing the soil surface will likely plant a host of annual weeds. Try to leave as much residue on the soil surface as possible to protect against erosion.

If you are going to do a late spring or early summer planting, eliminating weeds should be taken seriously prior to planting. If the selected site does not contain heavy stands of perennial weeds and was previously in soybeans or corn, till the soil by shallow disking or field cultivation every three weeks beginning in late April; this will eliminate many weed problems. Follow up the final disking with a field harrow to level the field and break up clods; then roll the soil using a cultipacker or corrugated cast-iron field roller. Rolling provides a good, firm seedbed and is your best defense against erosion. Keep in mind that any tillage may open up the soil for erosion should heavy spring rains occur.

If the area contains newly emerging annual weeds or a heavy stand of smooth brome grass, reed canary grass, quack grass, Canada thistle, or other undesirable perennial plants, consider spraying the emergent green vegetation with the herbicide Roundup (glyphosate). This will prevent serious problems later. Plants must be actively growing; if they are perennials, use three to four quarts of Roundup per acre. Roundup is not a restricted pesticide, although you will need to take precautions to avoid spraying any desirable plants. We have occasionally covered plants with a bag during spraying to prevent damage to them. The most effective treatments have been done in late fall, when plants are storing food reserves in their roots. Previous herbicide use on cropland has not proved to be a serious problem.

CHAPTER SIX

OLD PASTURE SEEDING

What is the procedure for seeding an old pasture? Are there any benefits?

If you're thinking about establishing prairie in an old pasture, here are some recommendations. Before doing anything to the site, take an inventory of what is growing there. We purchased an eighty-acre pasture fourteen years ago, and during the summer before we took possession we were able to make a list of nearly one hundred native species that were growing on the site. Generally it is best to allow the pasture vegetation to grow for at least a year after a history of heavy grazing to see what shows up. Burning the area may activate bonsai prairie plants. Our site had been so

⌃ Black-eyed Susan, daisy fleabane, and hoary vervain
in the fifth or sixth year of a pasture restoration.

overgrazed that it took three years before we had enough vegetation to do the first burn.

Here is a procedure that we used that you might try if parts of your pasture are extremely degraded. First, we mowed the area in October and waited until new green vegetation appeared. We then sprayed it with Roundup in early November.

If the site had been smooth enough to drive over with a mower the next summer, we would have fall-seeded in late November. Instead, in early April, we burned off the dead vegetation. A few weeks later, remnant stands of big bluestem, side-oats grama, prairie violet, and sedges came up green and lively. They had been untouched by the spraying since they were in a dormant state. We tilled the soil lightly where there were native plants. We used a field cultivator in the rest of the area to uproot the rhizomes in patches of reed canary grass and an extensive area of smooth brome. Once the ground was leveled, we rolled it with a cultipacker and spread the seed mix.

Through the summer following the seeding, we mowed the area several times to a height of three or four inches to control weed growth. In reality weeds make a good cover crop if you keep them short enough that they do not smother the new prairie seedlings.

In other parts of our pasture site, we did fall overseeding without any ground preparation. No mowing, no herbicide, and for the most part no fire. The seed that we spread consisted primarily of early successional species such as gray-headed coneflower, saw-tooth sunflower, cup plant, ox-eye, and small amounts of native grasses. The results have been phenomenal. Many weedy species such as Queen Anne's lace have nearly disappeared. The bands of color from the overseeded species follow the line of the meandering stream across a rich bottomland.

We did a considerable amount of overseeding on the site in the winter months. In the spring of our thirteenth year of ownership, a wildfire burned a large portion of it. That summer we saw numerous prairie plants that had never been visible before.

In some cases, it may have been seven or eight years before plants in the seeded area bloomed for the first time. Remember that your goal is to displace the bad stuff with the good stuff. In every case, try to be patient; prairies are largely composed of perennial plants. They are long-lived with full root development and succession occurring gradually over a decade or longer. Persistent attention will be needed for years to come.

CHAPTER SEVEN

SEEDING

What kinds of equipment will work best? How much seed should you plant?
Is there a best time to seed?

There is no perfect time to seed tallgrass prairie. Successful plantings have been done in spring, summer, and fall. For many years we planted in mid to late June and found that we had fewer weed problems than we encountered with early spring seedings. There is also less chance of erosion from very heavy spring rains after mid June.

Since some species of forbs need cold-wet stratification to germinate, they may not germinate until the following spring. Cold-wet stratification means that the seed

⌃ Drop seeders such as this old Ezee Flow fertilizer
spreader work well for many seeding applications.

needs to be moist and just above freezing for a period of thirty to ninety days to break its dormancy. This process occurs over winter when you seed in late October and early to mid November and appears to give a wider variety of species an equal start. On some occasions we have planted the first half of the seed in the fall and overseeded the second half, without tillage, the following fall. Seed harvested from native stands usually varies considerably in quantity, quality, and species diversity from one season to the next. To increase diversity in your planting, use seed that is harvested in two different crop years.

Seed about ten to fifteen pounds of mixed forbs and grasses per acre using at least twice the weight of forbs compared to that of grass seed. Use a ten-pound rate for certified seed and a fifteen-pound rate for hand-collected seed. We use a rate of fifteen pounds for seed harvested from virgin sites. Certified seed that has been tested for germination and purity is more reliable. It is, however, more expensive if you are planting for high species diversity.

Depending on the management of the native site, the viability of seed harvested from virgin stands can range from less than 10 to more than 70 percent. In any case, we have never had a planting failure when using a rate of fifteen pounds per acre. Regular burning on the harvest site is extremely important if you want to maintain seed quality and quantity from one year to the next. Sites that have not been burned for many years are generally poor seed producers (see chapter 10).

Truax and Great Plains drills work very well for clean seed; however, they may not work well with seed that contains broken leaves, large stems, and other debris larger than an inch. We have found that dry fertilizer spreaders work well for seed mixed with heavy trash, but the material must be agitated by a person riding in the back of the spreader or it will bridge up and fail to deliver a uniform quantity. Fertilizer spreaders distribute seed over an area about six feet wide. Ezee Flow spreaders work very well for seed that contains heavy trash. Three-point broadcast seeders such as the Vicon are also being used by many individuals with good results. After the seed is broadcast or drilled, harrow lightly if the soil has been cultivated and roll until the soil is very firm. Remember that rolling is your best defense against water erosion when the soil is not protected by vegetation. If you are planting on a soybean or corn stubble field, leave the seed on the surface and let natural weather conditions plant it.

A cultipacker or field roller is an important tool where the soil has been deeply disturbed by tillage. It will compact the soil to give a firm seedbed and help prevent erosion from heavy rainfall.

HELPFUL HERBICIDES

Are herbicides necessary? When can they be safely applied?

The challenges of establishing and maintaining reconstructed or restored prairie communities at times require every tool at your disposal. If you have a backyard garden, your hoe may be all that you need, but if you are working with more than a few acres, hand-weeding is often out of the question for some problem plants.

Thus, many land managers find the judicious use of herbicides an effective way to approach persistent problem plants, most of which are exotic species. We have observed that the use of herbicides, in a timely manner, causes very little if any damage

⌃ Field sprayers are important for treating large areas of perennial grasses such as reed canary and smooth brome, extensive patches of Canada thistle, and invasive legumes such as red clover.

to the prairie community. Every species has an Achilles' heel; when you determine what its weakness is, you will find hope instead of despair.

First, I would like to point out that, in most cases, low species diversity enters into the picture. Problem plants are also often apparent during the early stages of prairie succession, when abundant underground root space is still available. Weedy species may appear from the seed bank or emerge from active rhizomes present in the previous plant community. It is always easier to plant a prairie in a clean crop field than on land that was previously covered by perennial grasses and pasture legumes. This does not mean that you should till up prairie remnants in hopes of improving them, but be aware that it is not easy to transform old pastures into diverse and dynamic prairie communities.

The most commonly used herbicide in prairie restoration is glyphosate, with a trade name of Roundup. It is a systemic nonselective pesticide; that is, it translocates to the root system and kills actively growing green plants. Generally Roundup is used prior to planting to eliminate perennial grasses such as smooth brome, reed canary, and fescue or legumes such as red clover, crown vetch, and alfalfa or other undesirable species such as Canada thistle. It is not residual, which means it does not affect seeds on the ground or the growth of new seedlings.

Advertising leads us to believe that once we spray weeds, they are gone from the site. This sounds good, yet rarely is it as simple as it sounds since dormant seeds and active root rhizomes often remain in the soil. This is true not only with grasses but more so with legumes such as red clover, black medic, bird's-foot trefoil, and crown vetch, whose hard seed coats enable them to stay viable in the soil seed bank and germinate months or even years later.

Obviously, once you have seeded in your prairie and it has begun to emerge, you do not want to spray with Roundup or you will have to start all over. Oddly enough, this is both true and false. Certainly you do not want to kill your emerging prairie plants. During the first three years in the establishment process, spraying with Roundup at any time of the year is extremely risky. However, after your plants are well established and have flowered, using Roundup in late fall is a very effective way to control legumes such as red clover and crown vetch and exotic cool-season grasses such as smooth brome, reed canary, orchard grass, and fescue as well as Canada thistle. You can do this safely because prairie species go into a state of dormancy in mid October, when the chlorophyll shuts down photosynthesis. At this time of year, Roundup will do no harm to living but dormant prairie vegetation.

Most broadleaf plants can be killed with LV-4, better known as 2,4-D. Don't confuse this with DDT, the banned insecticide. LV stands for low volatility, which means that this herbicide does not drift into adjacent fields. It is relatively inexpensive and quite effective on thistles and most annuals. Another broadleaf herbicide is

Stinger, which is very effective on Canada thistle and legumes. 2,4-D does not seem to work well in late fall with low temperatures.

We have sprayed Roundup during the first three weeks of November on numerous occasions; while action of the herbicide is slow due to low temperatures, it has worked very well. In some areas we have almost completely eliminated smooth brome grass, red clover, and reed canary grass. Native prairie species quickly fill the empty spaces, and the prairie community becomes more resistant to future invasion. This process generally must be carried out several years in succession, coupled with prescribed fire to remove the offending seed bank.

Another commonly used herbicide is Select, which is designed to control annual grasses in soybeans. It is selective for grasses only, will not affect broadleaf plants, and can be used to set back smooth brome, fescue, or reed canary grass in an establishing prairie. The key to its effectiveness is using a perennial grass rate and applying it before native warm-season grasses begin to grow. Exotic perennial grasses are usually not eradicated, but they are set back several months in seasonal

⌃ Garden or spot sprayers are important for treating small areas of perennial grasses such as reed canary and smooth brome and problem broad-leaved plants such as red clover and Canada thistle.

growth, eliminating flowers and seed production for the growing season. As a result, desirable natives gain a growth advantage. This process can be very helpful when you are working with old pastures or degraded remnants. Another positive for Select is that it does not affect sedges.

Timing and the rate applied are critical with most herbicides. Be sure to check with a certified agricultural supplier before using them. These suppliers can tell you whether you need a surfactant (a wetting agent) or an additive such as ammonium sulfate, as well as how many gallons of water you should apply per acre to get effective control.

Consult the charts for our recommended herbicides and their uses. Use all herbicides with care, use protective equipment, and avoid spraying on windy days when the spray drift can affect nontargeted areas. Always follow directions on the label.

Problem Species and Suggested Herbicide Usage

Problem Species	Treatment	Herbicides	Timing	Comments
ANNUALS/BIENNIALS				
Velvetleaf or buttonweed Foxtail species Pigweed species Smartweed species Musk, bull, tall, and field thistles	Tillage prior to planting may be best unless the potential for erosion is a serious concern.	Roundup works for all. LV-4 works only for broadleaves. Select works for foxtail.	Best results occur if plants are 5 to 12 inches high.	Annual broadleaf plants generally disappear the second year after planting; thistles are biennial and persist only a couple of years. Mowing or hand-weeding may be best.
PERENNIALS				
Grasses: reed canary, smooth brome, bluegrass, and quack grass	Tillage may break up the rhizomes of grasses and weaken them, but they often regrow. Herbicide applications are more effective in most cases, but they will not deal with viable seed that remains in the soil.	Roundup is a contact herbicide that will kill perennial grasses. Select is very effective in reducing the vigor and seed set of invading cool-season perennial grasses such as brome and reed canary.	Grasses must be actively growing for Roundup to work effectively. Application rates generally need to be higher in spring than in fall.	It appears that late fall applications are far more effective than those in spring since the plants are storing food in their roots at this time.

Problem Species and Suggested Herbicide Usage

Problem Species	Treatment	Herbicides	Timing	Comments
Canada thistle	Broadleaf herbicides work best but probably will not eliminate the problem.	Stinger is a broadleaf herbicide that works very well and will not kill grasses. Roundup is nonselective and should be used only prior to planting.	Plants must be actively growing. Herbicides can be applied throughout the season, but late fall applications seem to be more effective.	Canada thistle is generally crowded out in very diverse plantings by the fourth or fifth season. Cutting or pulling in the bloom stage is very effective.
Curly dock	Use tillage or broadleaf herbicides prior to planting.	Use Roundup, Stinger, or LV-4.	Apply before plants have a flower or seed stalk.	Curly dock is present in most fields; however, it tends to diminish in size and vigor as the planting grows older with or without treatment.
LEGUMES				
Sweet clovers (Yellow sweet clover is usually biennial. White sweet clover can be either biennial or annual.)	All broadleaf herbicides work on sweet clover.	Use Roundup, Stinger, or LV-4.	Use tillage or a broadleaf herbicide prior to planting. In an established planting, hand-weed or mow large concentrations in the bloom stage.	Apply when plants are actively growing. Try to prevent plants from setting seed. Seed from sweet clover may live for years in the seed bank and is fire-scarified; thus new infestations often appear the year after a burn.

Red clover	All broadleaf herbicides work on red clover during the growing season.	Use Roundup, Stinger, or LV-4. For late fall applications in cold weather only, Roundup will work effectively.	In old fields prior to planting, apply before seed sets. In established plantings, after prairie goes dormant (usually in mid October), spray the area with Roundup in November. Note that prairie forbs in a young planting do not go dormant until a hard freeze.	We have found fall treatments to be very effective; however, you need to follow up the procedure for several successive years while burning annually to germinate and remove old seed.
Alsike clover Dutch white clover	Broadleaf herbicides or tillage will remove actively growing stands of these species, but viable seed will remain in the soil.	Use Roundup, Stinger, or LV-4.	Important: Do not spray in newly established plantings or you will kill emerging prairie seedlings.	Generally, both species are not a problem in well-established diverse plantings. They gradually disappear over time.

Problem Species and Suggested Herbicide Usage

Problem Species	Treatment	Herbicides	Timing	Comments
Crown vetch Bird's-foot trefoil	Broadleaf herbicides will remove actively growing stands of these species; however, viable seed will remain in the soil. Crown vetch is by far the most serious of the two since it spreads by runners and intertwines with other species. The goal of control is to stop seed production by removing blooming plants.	Use Roundup, Stinger, or LV-4. Be aware that this will also remove broadleaf prairie plants. Note: In established plantings use Stinger or LV-4 during the growing season.	In well-established prairie stands, mow after dormancy (mid October) and spray with Roundup in November.	The effects of Roundup treatments done in November are barely visible but very effective. Bird's-foot trefoil has a taproot and can be dug with a spade if you have only a few plants. As with all legumes, hard seed will remain viable for years and seedlings will emerge after fire scarification.

Herbicides, Active Ingredients, and Generic Equivalents

Usage	Nonselective: Grass and Broadleaf	Grass Only	Broadleaf Only
Herbicides	Roundup, by Monsanto	Select, by Arysta LifeScience	Stinger and Milestone, by Dow AgroSciences LLC
Active Ingredient	Glyphosate	Clethodim	Aminopyralid, Clopyralid
Generic Equivalents	Buccaneer, by TENKŌZ Gly-Star Plus, by Agri Star Rodeo (aquatic), by Monsanto Roundup ProDry and Honcho, by Monsanto	Volunteer, by TENKŌZ Intensity One, by Loveland Products Fusilade DX, by Syngenta Crop Protection, LLC	Lo-Vol 4 and Lo-Vol 6 (2,4-D), by TENKŌZ

Tables adapted with permission from *Woodlands and Prairies Magazine*, www.woodlandsandprairiesmagazine.com.

CHAPTER NINE

POSTPLANTING MOWING

Will mowing control most weeds? What kinds of mowers are best?
How often should you mow a new planting?

Our postplanting mowing begins when annual weeds have grown twelve to fifteen inches high after a summer planting. If the seed was planted in the fall, you will need to start mowing in early to mid June.

Summer weed pressure on previously cultivated cropland will likely consist of lamb's quarters, velvetleaf or buttonweed, pigweed, yellow and giant foxtail, common and giant ragweed, nightshade, and smartweed. Mowing to a height of three or

⌃ Rotary mowers such as this Woods work well for the first stages of growth.
They can be raised to cut above the growing prairie plants.

four inches should continue at three-week intervals for the first month to six weeks. Then raise your mower to six inches in height until weed pressure subsides, usually in late August or early September. If weed pressure is very heavy, a three-inch mowing height may be necessary for the entire summer.

If there is adequate rainfall, emerging plants of purple prairie clover, gray-headed coneflower, stiff goldenrod, and compass plant will be two to three inches high in six to eight weeks. Grasses will also begin to emerge and will be four to six inches high. We have found six-inch compass plants in early June from a fall seeding in early November. The leaves on newly emerging prairie grasses are very fine and wispy compared to foxtail and are easy to overlook. If you happen to mow the tops of taller plants, they will keep growing. Keep in mind that unbridled weed growth during this six- to eight-week period may exceed four feet in height. We have often seen foxtail,

⋏ Sickle mowers are more energy efficient when mowing large plantings.
They can also be adjusted to cut above the growing vegetation.

38

lamb's quarters, and smartweed exceed one hundred individuals per square foot. Sunlight at ground level under a heavy weed canopy will be greatly reduced, and if there is less than adequate rainfall, seedlings may be unable to get enough moisture. Some seeds may not germinate if there is excessive weed pressure.

Using a sickle-type mower may speed up mowing, although it lays down a layer of green vegetation as opposed to the shredding action of a rotary mower. This material will dry and wither in about twenty-four hours and make little impact on the emerging plants. Be careful not to bunch up material when turning the mower as heavy piles can smother small seedlings. However, this is a very minor problem in a large-scale planting. Windrows left by rotary mowers can also be a problem if the vegetation is heavy.

Postplanting mowing helps give plants an equal start. Seedlings needing more light for development seem to compete better with those that have wider light tolerances for germination and growth.

On some prairie reconstructions, many plants appear as isolated specimens. Our plantings have given us the opposite result. A few plants may appear as isolated specimens, but most appear equally distributed throughout the planting depending on their moisture requirements. Each species is represented not by dozens of specimens but by hundreds, thousands, or tens of thousands of individuals.

Without mowing to control weedy competition, easily established species such as big bluestem, black-eyed Susan, saw-tooth sunflower, and gray-headed coneflower may eventually dominate. This can create a plant community with low species diversity and long-term instability. In the end, mowing encourages higher species diversity, more spaces are filled, and a more stable plant community results. This postseeding weed control is the most important part of a successful establishment, especially in a dry year when the lack of moisture may be a limiting factor.

Although we generally mow only during the first season, we have often mowed an established planting during the second growing season as well. Why some plantings begin growth in six to eight weeks and others take eighteen months is a mystery. On several occasions it has taken until the middle of the second season before we began to see emerging plants; thus, we used a six-inch mowing height all of the second season.

Do not fertilize your planting with nitrogen. Research from the University of Minnesota indicates that high levels of nitrogen may be detrimental to prairies. Tissue culture studies of prairie-fringed orchids by Marge From at the University of Nebraska at Omaha indicate that plants may be inhibited from germinating because excess nitrogen in the soil destroys essential fungal activity. The fine, hairlike hyphae of the fungi penetrate the seed coat to provide nutrients for embryonic development. Most prairie seeds have a stored source of food for embryonic growth, so this is not an issue. We are certain, however, that high nitrate levels encourage excessive weed growth. The competition from weedy annuals that results can make prairie establishment very difficult.

Second-season mowings on stands that are established appear to help control species such as curly dock, smooth brome and reed canary grass, and yellow and white sweet clovers. Generally we set the mower at a cutting height of six to eight inches. If curly dock is cut when the seed head is at its maximum height, it will exhibit only a short regrowth. Smooth brome and reed canary grass cut in the bloom stage fail to put up a second flower stalk, so cutting these species can favor the establishing prairie plants.

John Judson from near Dedham, Iowa, has told me that he has on some occasions mowed newly established plantings during the third growing season and has seen positive effects from the process. Dave Williams, the program manager for the Prairie Institute at the Tallgrass Prairie Center in Cedar Falls, Iowa, did extensive research on the effects of mowing for his master's thesis. He found that frequent mowing in the first season after sowing new forb species into an established grassland can have a profound impact on the plant community well into the future: increased forb abundance, increased forb richness, and a more diverse plant community with dominant native prairie grasses.

CHAPTER TEN

FIRE IN TALLGRASS PRAIRIE

Why is fire used in prairie management? What are its negative influences?
Can management be done without fire?

Fire stimulates growth and development and can be used as early as the beginning
of the third growing season. The prairie without fire quickly becomes unstable and
gradually changes to woodland. Fire is a disturbance, but a necessary one if a prairie
is to remain a prairie. Because the growing points of most plants are below the soil
surface in early spring, they are protected from fire. Those who have watched a grassland fire know it moves quickly, with little heat penetrating below the soil surface.

⌃ Mowed and raked firebreaks and a drip torch make the process of prairie burning easier and safer. 41

Prairie reconstructions can respond to the positive effects of fire as soon as the second year. However, it may be difficult to burn a newly established prairie because its fuel load may not be adequate.

Generally, burns should be conducted in the spring between March and late April. Late April is better for controlling cool-season grasses such as brome and bluegrass, although this depends on the growth stage of the plants.

Burning may increase the root biomass of a prairie, which is generally two to four times greater than the aboveground biomass. This occurs since burning stimulates the production of new leaves, which is the result of increased tillering.

Because fire opens up the soil surface to increased sunlight and heat, earlier growth and development occur. Unless soil conditions are very dry, our observations indicate that grasses and forbs are not only taller but produce more flowers when they are burned. Anecdotal research indicates that a standing crop of warm-season grasses can be increased threefold with fire. Burned production fields produce more seed of higher quality. Decreased flowering of some species such as purple prairie clover and shooting star may occur after fire. These increases or decreases depend on the habitat, time of the burn, and available moisture.

Although it is commonly believed that fire prevented trees from invading prairies, it is difficult to eradicate established trees because only the tops of trees such as mulberry and sumac are usually killed by fire. When they resprout, three or more trunks often replace one, and initial problems become more difficult. Burning followed by cutting and treating the stumps with herbicides such as Crossbow prevents the problem from recurring. I have found that most trees get started when the prairie is young, usually in the first or second year. Once prairie plant root systems are formed, tree establishment generally does not present a serious problem except in the case of quaking aspen and sumac, which form clones that begin with a single tree. Litter removal by haying or light grazing may control trees where fire cannot be used.

Some animals respond positively to fire and increase in numbers following a burn. Other animals may be eliminated by fire and need to recolonize the area. Mosaic burns that leave patches of burned and unburned ground benefit the greatest number of species. Light grazing prevents the accumulation of litter in some areas and tends to promote a mosaic burn pattern.

I remember seeing very large numbers of meadow voles following a burn on an area that had not been burned the two previous years. Occasionally we find deer mice, shrews, and voles killed by fire; however, most appear to escape. After a prairie is established, a two- or three-year burn cycle will give those that respond to fire and those that do not an equal advantage. In most cases, mammals recolonize areas to preburn levels in two to three years.

Much concern has been expressed regarding the loss of invertebrates such as butterflies with the use of fire. Fire often appears to have consumed all existing vegetation, although this is rarely the case. We have observed that fast-moving fires burn over the surface of lodged grasses. Tall grasses and flowers may burn off at ground level, yet the stalks remain unburned. The mosaic effect of prairie fire in part explains how insects survived the presettlement fires that burned over large areas. Burning

⌃ Using a field sprayer, you can effectively put down a wet line to control a backfire to create a firebreak. Once a head fire starts, it is very difficult to control the speed of the burn.

only portions of your prairie in any given year will enable species intolerant of fire to find refuge in the unburned areas. Research conducted by Nancy Slife on leafhoppers in the prairie indicated that fire increases species diversity.

I believe that annual burning during the first ten years is very beneficial. New seedling emergence following fire gives dramatic evidence of the positive effect it has on a prairie's dynamic properties, meaning that the community continues to diversify and will remain healthy for the greatest number of plants and animals.

CHAPTER ELEVEN

GROWTH AND DEVELOPMENT

How long until my prairie is mature? Does species diversity affect long-term stability?
Why is it important to be patient?

It is important to understand that considerable time is required for prairie to develop from seed to seedlings to a mature successional stage. Plantings that appear to be failures during the first two years can turn out very well.

The first year of growth for most plantings rarely shows promise. Since seedlings first put down an extensive root system, they are difficult to find during the first weeks and months. In drier than normal years, there may be little or no visible

⌃ In early morning light, we see a planting in the third growing season that contains a profusion of species like gray-headed coneflower and Canada wild rye. Early successional species diminish as the planting ages and diversifies.

45

growth the first season. Plant development that should have taken place the first year may not take place until the second.

We seeded one of our plantings in late June of 1988. A summer of drought followed, and we saw only bare dirt with a few weeds. We kept the weed growth trimmed to a height of two to four inches. The following year was nearly as dry; however, as the growing season progressed, we gradually moved the mowing height up to six inches. In August of 1989, we began to see a sprinkling of side-oats grama and wispy strands of purple prairie clover scattered throughout the planting. During these first two years, the prognosis was bleak, but by the summer of 1990 a wide diversity of species was scattered throughout the planting. Foxtail was still predominant, but the prairie plants were winning the battle.

The planting covered about one acre. In its sixth growing season, it was virtually weed-free and had a dense cover of more than forty species of flowers and grasses. During its seventh growing season, compass plants and white wild indigo began to flower throughout the stand. Because it is a dry site, cup plant and New England aster, which require mesic to wet conditions, disappeared. This section of our prairie is now twenty-three years old and continues to change its species composition. Tall grasses are gradually displacing shorter prairie grasses, while the number of forbs may be increasing. It appears that a succession of wet springs and summers also has had an effect in shifting the balance toward taller grasses and away from those species that prefer dry sites.

In years when rainfall is normal, many plants will establish during the first growing season. Fall plantings are nearly always a season ahead of spring or early summer plantings. This apparently occurs because winter provides a cold-wet stratification period. Some prairie forbs require this treatment for a period of thirty to sixty days in order to germinate.

Where weed control has not been practiced, seedlings can be lost during the first growing season due to weedy competition. This depends on the amount of weed pressure and available moisture. In dry years, the problem is more serious. The loss of light due to shading from a dense overstory of weedy vegetation also limits seedling growth and may crowd out seedlings altogether. Species such as lamb's quarters, giant ragweed, and giant foxtail can exceed five feet in height during the

growing season. Where there are serious infestations, the number of plants may exceed one hundred per square foot, and prairie species that are sensitive to competition may be wiped out altogether.

Plantings with low species diversity and few individuals leave openings for weed infestation and subsequent long-term problems. During the drought of 1988, I watched a forty-acre switchgrass planting where some areas were mowed and others were not. The mowed areas had a good seedling survival rate; the unmowed areas had a 100 percent seedling loss. The young plants died from lack of moisture due to

⌃ New seedlings are small and may be difficult to detect in the early stages of growth because of annual weeds and grasses. Starting from the upper left and going clockwise are new plants of wild bergamot, thimbleweed, pale purple coneflower, and partridge pea.

the demands from weedy competition. Nearly two-thirds of the planting had to be reseeded the following year.

During the second growing season, many individual plants will appear, provided weed control has been practiced. The second season of growth has a number of different weed problems. Lamb's quarters, smartweed, pigweed, velvetleaf, and foxtail generally decrease measurably since they require disturbance for reestablishment. Weedy biennial and perennial plants take over as annuals disappear.

In some plantings, the second growing season might be called the curly dock season, since this rank plant often appears in large numbers, much as it might in a first-year legume stand of alfalfa or red clover. It is often accompanied by white and yellow sweet clovers, red clover, Queen Anne's lace, bull thistle, Canada thistle, tall thistle (a native species that can appear to be out of control in this stage of establishment), and the occasional burdock. If the area is not too large and the plants are not too numerous, these species should be hand-weeded.

Canada thistle gradually diminishes in number and vigor as the planting becomes more established. We have spot-treated individual plants with a 30 percent Roundup solution but found that we did considerable damage to adjacent plants. This apparently occurs because Roundup vaporizes in warm weather and subsequently moves on to adjacent vegetation. Pulling mature plants when they are in the bloom stage can severely weaken an established clone—be sure to use leather gloves. In some cases, where the prairie community is developing well, we have noticed little difference in Canada thistle numbers at the end of the season regardless of whether we removed them, treated them with herbicide, or ignored them. Simply put, they cannot survive competition from diverse, healthy, deep-rooted prairie plants. Bull thistle will disappear by the third or fourth year without management provided there is good species diversity. Tall thistle assumes a more normal distribution, occurring only where there are minor disturbances.

If not controlled, yellow and white sweet clovers will become more abundant. Although they do not appear to crowd out native plants, they are serious pests. White sweet clover is both annual and biennial; yellow sweet clover appears to be only biennial. First-year seedlings of sweet clovers often go unnoticed in the understory. Control of sweet clovers can be accomplished by mowing them in the early flowering stage if the number of plants is too great to hand-weed. Late spring burning may also control them. This procedure, however, can be difficult due to inadequate dry plant material for fuel and green vegetation that will not burn. Burning also scarifies the seeds of sweet clovers and encourages germination. Both controls, late spring burning to kill young plants and mowing plants in the bloom stage, need to be practiced for a number of successive years.

Curly dock decreases in number when the prairie has sufficient diversity. The dock plants gradually shrink in height and vigor until only a few plants are present in five- and six-year-old plantings. Generally, we mow the seed heads off curly dock in early summer during the second and third growing seasons by setting the mower at a height of eight to ten inches. This seems to help weaken the plants and reduce seed production.

In the third and fourth growing seasons, gray-headed coneflower, stiff goldenrod, and saw-tooth sunflower dominate the stand to provide a spectacular summer show. Gray-headed coneflowers gradually decrease in abundance after the fourth season. Saw-tooth sunflowers shorten in height due to root competition from other species and assume their rank stature only on the edge of the planting, where they tend to be a colonizer. Grasses such as big and little bluestem and forbs such as purple prairie clover, leadplant, prairie blazing star, tall cinquefoil, pale purple coneflower, and compass plant gradually assume a dominant presence in the plant community.

The fourth growing season usually marks the beginning of a nearly weed-free prairie plant community. This occurs only where there is adequate species diversity and many individuals representing each species equally scattered throughout the planting. We have often harvested about fifty pounds of seed per acre from four-year-old plantings.

Plantings that have low species diversity and lack large numbers of individuals are generally plagued by problems from weedy species such as Canada thistle, sweet clovers, wild parsnip, and tall thistle, which thrive in openings and disturbances. Without enough competition, many desirable plants will establish themselves as small colonies or clones of single species, which will create a very unstable plant community.

One of our plantings, now nearly thirty-eight years old, looked quite weed-free

during the first fifteen years. At age twenty the entire planting began to lose its structural integrity and was beset by a host of problems. Most desirable species appeared only as isolated individuals in a stand of showy sunflower and a southwestern cultivar of switchgrass. Big bluestem, which once covered the entire site, gradually disappeared over a period of ten years (perhaps due to a fungal disease), and switchgrass became the dominant grass. Big bluestem then began to return, along with an increasing predominance of Indian grass. The planting now has relatively high species diversity, with many individuals of most species. Queen Anne's lace has nearly disappeared. The changes began after we interseeded the stand with a diverse species mix in 1997. The effect of a diverse adjacent planting is also readily apparent. A wave of change moves farther across it each year.

Plantings more than five years old with good species diversity and numerous

⌃ After seventeen years of growth, a rich and diverse mosaic of native species has developed in this planting. Annual spring burns have taken place every year starting in its fourth growing season.

individuals of each species begin to exhibit dynamic properties. Prairie plants that are not site-adapted gradually disappear. Few individual plants turn into clones, and species that do clone, such as prairie cord grass, will be mixed with blue flag iris, swamp milkweed, blue vervain, and bottle gentian. Empty spaces are quickly occupied by prairie colonizers, such as gray-headed coneflower, golden alexanders, stiff goldenrod, and saw-tooth sunflower, instead of weedy disturbance species.

A number of species may take more than four years to flower. The most notable in our plantings are white wild indigo and compass plant. White wild indigo, which has a tall white spike of flowers, may begin flowering in the fifth or sixth year but will not assume its stately stature for a number of years after its first flowering. Compass plants that may bloom in just a couple of years in a garden setting will generally take four or five years to bloom when they are surrounded by competition from other prai-

▲ A dense stand of pale purple coneflower, black-eyed Susan, and round-
headed bush-clover in a thirty-year-old prairie reconstruction.

rie species. I once planted some rootstock in a well-established reconstruction, and twelve years passed before they put up their first flower stalks. Compass plants seem to thrive in diverse environments. I have found them flowering on the rocky ridges of goat prairies and in prairie swales only a yard or two from blue flag iris but have not seen them growing on sand prairies.

After more than thirty-five seasons of prairie plantings and management, I conclude that a mature prairie community is a relative term. Changes in the frequency and distribution of species continue indefinitely. This seems to be a reflection of the initial species diversity, management regime, and soil and moisture conditions that may be indirectly linked to long-term weather patterns.

CHAPTER TWELVE

QUESTIONS AND ANSWERS

How can I eliminate a pure stand of reed canary grass, smooth brome grass, silver plume or pampas grass, or switchgrass prior to planting or control it in an established site?

You can first try to curtail seed production of these species through the process of summer haying or constant mowing. This should be followed by an application of Roundup, applied at a rate of at least three quarts of Roundup to twenty gallons of water per acre. This will kill the root systems. Late fall applications seem to be the most effective because the plants are storing food reserves in the roots then. Deep tillage may be helpful, but moldboard plowing will generally not eliminate these species. Planting a very diverse seed mixture, frequent burning, and follow-up

˄ Birds such as the dickcissel use flower stalks such as this compass plant for singing perches to defend their territories. They are abundant breeding birds in a well-developed prairie community.   53

applications of Select (a cool-season grass herbicide) in spring will reduce the vigor of cool-season grasses and help prairie species gain a competitive advantage.

We have found that you cannot completely eradicate reed canary grass; however, if you have high species diversity and utilize fire, it will become part of the natural community and will be controlled by other native wetland species. Diversity will also control switchgrass and prevent the overly aggressive nature that it exhibits when planted as a monoculture or in a planting with low species diversity.

Will the "Meadow in a Can" mixes currently on the market supply the correct species for a prairie planting?

No. Generally, these mixes have some prairie species, such as purple coneflower, exotic grassland species such as gaillardia and gold poppy, and garden varieties such as dame's rocket or bachelor button. They are designed for a quick and colorful garden but usually last only a year or two before needing to be replanted. They do not contain a good prairie matrix required for a long-term, stable plant community.

When mixed with native prairie species, the early flowering of these mixes may discourage the prairie planter from doing needed mowing to enhance the survivability of important species. Species such as dame's rocket make a quick show of color but are not adapted to the prairie plant community and gradually disappear. To sum it up, these mixes are designed for the average impatient gardener who is interested in immediate results. When purchasing any premixed seed, always look at the number of native species and the amounts of each species.

Will harvesting seed from a prairie planting or native prairie tract damage the site?

First, remember that most prairie species are either perennials or biennials, one exception being the annual partridge pea. Most species grow from established roots and have little dependence on seed to maintain plant populations. In well-established plantings, there is little root space available for new plants.

We generally harvest the majority of our prairie seed in the second week of October, when the green is gone from most of the plants and the stems and seed heads are dry. At this stage, the seed heads shatter easily, making it impossible to gather all the seeds from any individual plant. To date we have seen no negative effects on sites where seed harvests have been conducted year after year.

Can forbs be interseeded into a well-established stand of prairie grasses, or can prairie grasses be interseeded into a well-established stand of forbs?

Interseeding of forbs or grasses appears to work best when done in the early stages of a prairie planting, generally in the first two years. Keep in mind that, as underground root space becomes occupied by the established perennials, new seedlings will have greater difficulty gaining a foothold. However, we are also seeing that diversity appears to spread and integrate across even long-established plantings, provided there is active management by fire.

Will prairie plants invade neighboring crop fields?

Those of us who have a great fondness for prairies wish this were the case, since there would not be such a dramatic shortage of prairie plants across the Midwest today. Because the majority of prairie species are perennials and take from two to three years to establish, they cannot gain a foothold in cultivated fields and pose no problem for the agricultural community. Dogbane, common milkweed, and occasionally wild roses at one time persisted in cultivated fields, but these plants pose little or no threat to agriculture due to the use of broad-spectrum herbicides.

I once witnessed saw-tooth sunflowers invading the edge of a noncultivated field border. I believe the threat to the crop was largely cosmetic, but the farmer mowed the border and sprayed the adjoining roadside. Spraying on the field border would have killed the perceived threat and would not have eliminated the forbs in the adjacent roadside.

An increasing number of farmers are finding that diverse prairie plant communities provide excellent erosion control, good wildlife habitat, and a welcome relief from grass monocultures that lack long-term stability.

How does crown vetch enter into the picture?

Although crown vetch is an attractive plant when in flower, it appears to be the kudzu of the north. It is an invasive weed that should never have been planted, since it has little ability to control erosion or control the growth of noxious weeds. While crown vetch appears to cover the land, it only canopies, leaving the soil surface below barren and open to the erosive action of running water. Road banks, hidden from view, are deeply rilled.

Crown vetch does not possess the ground cover or underground root system needed to control the growth of many noxious weeds, such as giant ragweed, Canada thistle, and wild parsnip. Noxious weeds cannot be sprayed for control in crown vetch since it is susceptible to herbicides such as 2,4-D. Crown vetch also invades pastureland, natural areas, woodland edges, and other noncultivated fields.

Any type of grass stand will give better soil cover and will be more effective at erosion and weed control. A mix of prairie grasses and forbs will also provide far longer periods of roadside color in addition to providing better soil stability on steep slopes. Wildlife biologists generally concur that crown vetch makes poor wildlife habitat, since birds cannot walk through it as they can a grass stand.

Do not plant crown vetch under any circumstances. If it is near your prairie establishment area, make every effort to get rid of it before you begin planting. You can control it with light applications of 2,4-D (a rate of one quart per acre) in an established grassland or by using Roundup; however, this may take repeated applications over a period of several years and monitoring for many years in the future. Crown vetch can also present problems in the future since burning will scarify seed remaining in the ground and new seedlings will need to be treated.

We have been fighting crown vetch that invaded from a roadside planting for more than twenty years and still find small patches each year.

How do prairie plants control the growth of weeds, or does this really happen?

Prairie plant communities control the growth of both annual and perennial weeds by crowding them out. This occurs when the root systems of a diverse prairie plant matrix fill up the available root space. Good species diversity fills all available spaces above and below ground. It generally takes three to five years for a planting to develop to this point. We still find occasional Canada thistles in five-year-old plantings, but they are isolated individuals, usually one to two feet high, and rare in number after the third growing season. One must remember that diversity is an important part of the picture. The higher the species diversity, the more completely the root space will be filled and the less chance that you will have openings for weedy species.

How can I determine the quantity of seed in bulk material that has been combined or stripped?

From a representative portion of the bulk mix, separate a small amount (for example, a heaping tablespoon) to use as a sample. Separate the seed from the straw, seed hulls, flower parts, weed seed, etc. A hand lens and sharp-pointed tweezers are needed for this process, while a dissecting scope can be used to determine if the seeds are filled.

Weigh the two resulting elements of the sorting process, seed and foreign material, separately. A fine electronic scale works best; otherwise, a gunpowder scale works well. These scales are inexpensive. They will weigh very small sample sizes, which is a necessary feature since many prairie seeds are tiny and light in weight.

Add the weight of the seed and the foreign material together to get a total weight for the sample. Divide the sum weight of the seed by the total weight of the sample to get the percentage of seed in the bulk material. Example: If the seed weight is 37.5 grains and the foreign material weight is 61.1 grains, the total weight of the sample is 98.6 grains. Divide the seed weight of 37.5 by the total sample weight of 98.6, and you get a seed percentage of 38 percent.

How much seed can I expect to harvest from a prairie remnant or a good prairie planting?

We have found that the percentage of seed in a combined mix varies from .05 percent during a very poor seed year to 30 percent in a good year. Good prairie management with average rainfall and lots of sunlight usually produces an excellent seed crop. Generally our harvests from virgin prairies have averaged 6 to 7 percent seed, while those from our own plantings, which are less diverse species-wise, range from 16 to 30 percent. In terms of pounds per acre, virgin prairies produce about twenty pounds in a good year, and planted stands with sixty to seventy species will produce forty to a hundred pounds of actual seed. Bear in mind that large quantities of species such as compass plants can dramatically alter these figures.

As the prairie ages and develops, the species that make up the harvest change and seed production is affected. Generally speaking, as a planting gets older, the number of species harvested increases and the amount of actual seed in pounds per acre decreases.

Can the use of herbicides aid in the establishment process?

As previously mentioned, Roundup eliminates perennial grasses and broadleaf weeds such as Canada thistle prior to planting. Late fall applications seem to be the most effective for smooth brome grass, reed canary grass, and Canada thistle. I have also used fall applications of Roundup to control red clover. It must be applied several years in succession to get good results, coupled with annual spring burns to scarify and germinate old seed.

Select, made by Valent, was designed to control annual grasses such as foxtail in soybeans. This product is very effective in reducing the vigor and seed set of invading cool-season perennial grasses, such as brome and reed canary, and needs to be applied early in the spring before warm-season grasses emerge. It does not affect forbs but may stunt the growth of cool-season prairie natives such as Canada wild rye, June grass, or bluejoint.

See chapter 8 on herbicides and the tables at the end of that chapter for a complete list of herbicides and their use.

What is the best advice for a novice prairie restorationist?

Start small, use high seed diversity, have patience for development, and be able to follow up with good management. If you lack any of these key ingredients, you may compromise your success.

If I am buying land in the country what should I look for? What should I avoid?

There is an appeal to rolling pastureland. However, while it may have some remnant species, it is often far more difficult to reconstruct a viable prairie on pastureland because of the weed pressure than on a clean, cultivated crop field.

What are the long-term benefits of reconstructing a prairie?

Prairies provide some of the best wildlife habitat for a great diversity of animal species. Wetlands process nutrients such as nitrates to improve water quality. Soil structure is opened up after compaction from agricultural use to improve water-holding capacity. Soil erosion from a heavy rainfall is virtually halted. Aesthetically, prairies can provide color throughout the growing season.

An asterisk indicates that the supplier carries some or all local-ecotype seeds or plants.

Illinois

Art and Linda's Wildflowers★
Cicero IL 60804
708/785-2943
art@artandlindaswildflowers.com
www.artandlindaswildflowers.com

Bluestem Prairie Nursery★
Hillsboro IL 62049
217/532-6344
bluestemnursery@yahoo.com

Bottle gentians, rigid goldenrod, grass-leaved goldenrod, and the reddish stems of saw-tooth sunflowers are mixed with native grasses in a moist prairie swale in late August.

Earthskin Nursery*
Mason City IL 62664
217/482-3524
lrnelms@fgi.net
www.earthskinnursery.com

Genesis Nursery*
Tampico IL 61283
815/438-2220

Landscape Naturally, Inc.
Sycamore IL 60178
815/899-7574

Indiana

JFNew Native Plant Nursery
Walkerton IN 46574
574/586-2142
mobrien@jfnew.com
www.jfnew.com

Iowa

Allendan Seed Company*
Winterset IA 50273
515/462-1241
Allendan@handtech.com

Bratney Company
Urbandale IA 50322
515/270-2417
www.bratney.com

Broad View Wildflower Seed
Grinnell IA 50112
John@Broadviewwildflowerseed.com
Broadviewwildflowerseed.com

Diversity Farms*
Dedham IA 51440
712/683-5555
dfarms@pionet.net

Farber Bag and Supply Company
Peosta IA 52068
800/553-9068
baggs@mwci.net
www.farberbag.com

Ion Exchange*
Harpers Ferry IA 52146
800/291-2143
Hbright@IonXchange.com
www.ionxchange.com

Carl and Linda Kurtz*
St. Anthony IA 50239
641/477-8364
cpkurtz@netins.net

Osenbaugh Grass Seeds
Lucas IA 50151
800/582-2788

Swanson Farms*
Nevada IA 50201
515/382-6120
andy@midiowa.net

WildDesigns Landscaping
Centerville IA 52544
641/895-4846
brants09@yahoo.com

Michigan

Michigan Wildflower Farm*
Portland MI 48875
517/647-6010
wildflowers@voyager.net
www.michiganwildflowerfarm.com

Native Plant Nursery
Ann Arbor MI 48107
734/677-3260
plants@nativeplant.com
www.nativeplant.com

Minnesota

Feder's Prairie Seed Company*
Blue Earth MN 56013
feder@bevcomm.net
507/526-3049
www.federprairieseed.com

Mark E. Gullickson*
Fertile MN 56540
218/945-6894

Kaste Seed, Inc.*
Fertile MN 56540
218/945-6738

Morning Sky Greenery*
Morris MN 56267
320/795-6234
info@morningskygreenery.com
www.morningskygreenery.com

Prairie Hill Wildflowers*
Ellendale MN 56026
507/451-7791

Prairie Restorations, Inc.*
Princeton MN 55371
763/389-4342
info@prairieresto.com
www.prairieresto.com

Shooting Star Native Seeds*
Spring Grove MN 55974
507/498-3944
ssns@springgrove.coop
www.shootingstarnativeseed.com

Missouri

Hamilton Native Outpost
Elk Creek MO 65464
888/967-2190
natives@hamiltonnativeoutpost.com
www.hamiltonseed.com

Missouri Wildflowers Nursery
Jefferson City MO 65109
573/496-3492
mowldflrs@socket.net

Pure Air Native Seed Company
Novinger MO 63559
877/488-5531
oberle@PureAirSeed.com
www.pureairseed.com

Wisconsin

J & J Transplant Aquatic Nursery★
Wild Rose WI 54984
800/622-5055
jjtransplant@yahoo.com
www.tranzplant.com

Kettle Moraine Natural Landscaping★
Campbellsport WI 53010
www.kmnaturallandscaping.com

Prairie Seed Source★
North Lake WI 53064
pb9@PrairieBob.com
www.prairiebob.com

Equipment

Ag-Renewal, Inc.
Weatherford OK 73096
800/658-1446
ag-renewal@itlnet.net
http://ag-renewal.com

Farber Bag and Supply Company
Peosta IA 52068
800/553-9068
baggs@mwci.net
www.farberbag.com

Forestry Suppliers, Inc.
Jackson MS 39284
800/647-5368
www.forestry-suppliers.com

Prairie Habitats, Inc.
Argyle, Manitoba, Canada ROC OBO
204/467-9371
www.prairiehabitats.com

Truax Company, Inc.
New Hope MN 55430
763/537-6639
www.truaxcomp.com

REFERENCES

Christiansen, Paul, and Mark Müller. *An Illustrated Guide to Iowa Prairie Plants.* University of Iowa Press, 1999.

Dittmer, Lora, and Laura Jackson. *Prairie Seedlings Illustrated: An Identification Guide.* Vol. 1. University of Northern Iowa, 1997.

Eilers, Lawrence J., and Dean M. Roosa. *The Vascular Plants of Iowa: An Annotated Checklist and Natural History.* University of Iowa Press, 1994.

Helzer, Chris. *The Ecology and Management of Prairies in the Central United States.* University of Iowa Press, 2010.

Kurtz, Carl. *Iowa's Wild Places.* Iowa State University Press, 1996.

A male common yellowthroat in showy tick-trefoil. Yellowthroats are common nesters in tallgrass prairie.

Ladd, Doug, and Frank Oberle. *Tallgrass Prairie Wildflowers.* 2d ed. Falcon Press, 2005.

Madson, John. *Tallgrass Prairie.* Falcon Press, 1993.

Madson, John. *Where the Sky Began: Land of the Tallgrass Prairie.* Sierra Club Books, 1982; University of Iowa Press edition, 2004.

Mutel, Cornelia F. *The Emerald Horizon: The History of Nature in Iowa.* University of Iowa Press, 2008.

Packard, Stephen, and Cornelia F. Mutel, eds. *The Tallgrass Restoration Handbook: For Prairies, Savannas, and Woodlands.* Island Press, 1997.

Peterson, Roger Tory, and Margaret McKenny. *A Field Guide to Wildflowers of Northeastern and North-central North America.* Houghton Mifflin, 1968.

Rock, Harold. *Prairie Propagation Handbook.* Boerner Botanical Gardens, 1974.

Runkel, Sylvan T., and Dean M. Roosa. *Wildflowers and Other Plants of Iowa Wetlands.* Iowa State University Press, 1999.

Runkel, Sylvan T., and Dean M. Roosa. *Wildflowers of the Tallgrass Prairie: The Upper Midwest.* Iowa State University Press, 1989; 2d ed., University of Iowa Press, 2009.

Samson, Fred, and Fritz Knopf. *Prairie Conservation: Preserving North America's Most Endangered Ecosystem.* Island Press, 1996.

Shirley, Shirley. *Restoring the Tallgrass Prairie: An Illustrated Manual for Iowa and the Upper Midwest.* University of Iowa Press, 1994.

Smith, Daryl, Dave Williams, Greg Houseal, and Kirk Henderson. *The Tallgrass Prairie Center Guide to Prairie Restoration in the Upper Midwest.* University of Iowa Press, 2010.

Thompson, Janette R. *Prairies, Forests, and Wetlands: The Restoration of Natural Landscape Communities in Iowa.* University of Iowa Press, 1992.

Weaver, I. E. *Prairie Plants and Their Environment.* University of Nebraska Press, 1968.

Williams, Dave, and Brent Butler. *The Tallgrass Prairie Center Guide to Seed and Seedling Identification in the Upper Midwest.* University of Iowa Press, 2010.

Williams, Dave, Laura Jackson, and Daryl Smith. "Effects of Frequent Mowing on Survival and Persistence of Forbs Seeded into a Species-Poor Grassland." *Restoration Ecology* 15 (March 2007): 24–33.

Williams, Dave, Daryl Smith, Ryan Lensing, and Kathy Schultz. "Effects of Mowing on Abundance and Persistence of Tallgrass Prairie Forbs Seeded into an Established Stand of Prairie Grasses: Ten Years after Sowing." Proceedings of the 22d North American Prairie Conference: Restoration and Reconstruction, University of Northern Iowa Tallgrass Prairie Center, 2010.

OTHER BUR OAK BOOKS OF INTEREST

The Butterflies of Iowa
By Dennis W. Schlicht, John C. Downey, and Jeffrey Nekola

A Country So Full of Game: The Story of Wildlife in Iowa
By James J. Dinsmore

Deep Nature: Photographs from Iowa
Photographs by Linda Scarth and Robert Scarth, essay by John Pearson

The Ecology and Management of Prairies in the Central United States
By Chris Helzer

The Elemental Prairie: Sixty Tallgrass Plants
By George Olson and John Madson

The Emerald Horizon: The History of Nature in Iowa
By Cornelia F. Mutel

Enchanted by Prairie
By Bill Witt and Osha Gray Davidson

Field Guide to Wildflowers of Nebraska and the Great Plains
By Jon Farrar

Forest and Shade Trees of Iowa
By Peter J. van der Linden and Donald R. Farrar

The Guide to Oklahoma Wildflowers
By Patricia Folley

An Illustrated Guide to Iowa Prairie Plants
By Paul Christiansen and Mark Müller

The Iowa Breeding Bird Atlas
By Laura Spess Jackson, Carol A. Thompson, and James J. Dinsmore

The Iowa Nature Calendar
By Jean C. Prior and James Sandrock, illustrated by Claudia McGehee

Landforms of Iowa
By Jean C. Prior

Man Killed by Pheasant and Other Kinships
By John T. Price

Prairie: A North American Guide
By Suzanne Winckler

Prairie in Your Pocket: A Guide to Plants of the Tallgrass Prairie
By Mark Müller

Prairies, Forests, and Wetlands: The Restoration of Natural Landscape Communities in Iowa
By Janette R. Thompson

Restoring the Tallgrass Prairie: An Illustrated Manual for Iowa and the Upper Midwest
By Shirley Shirley

Stories from under the Sky
By John Madson

A Tallgrass Prairie Alphabet
By Claudia McGehee

The Tallgrass Prairie Center Guide to Prairie Restoration in the Upper Midwest
By Daryl Smith, Dave Williams, Greg Houseal, and Kirk Henderson

The Tallgrass Prairie Center Guide to Seed and Seedling Identification in the Upper Midwest
By Dave Williams and Brent Butler

The Vascular Plants of Iowa: An Annotated Checklist and Natural History
By Lawrence J. Eilers and Dean M. Roosa

Where the Sky Began: Land of the Tallgrass Prairie
By John Madson

Wildflowers of the Tallgrass Prairie: The Upper Midwest
By Sylvan T. Runkel and Dean M. Roosa